ANTONIN DVOÁÁK

QUARTET

for 2 Violins, Viola and Violoncello
C major/C-Dur/Ut majeur
Op. 61

T0081303

Ernst Eulenburg Ltd

London · Mainz · Madrid · New York · Paris · Prague · Tokyo · Toronto · Zürich

CONTENTS/INHALT

Ernst Eulenburg Ltd
48 Great Marlborough Street
London W1V 2BN

QUARTET

Antonín Dvořák
(1841–1904)
Op. 61
B 121

4

B

6

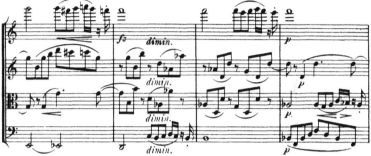

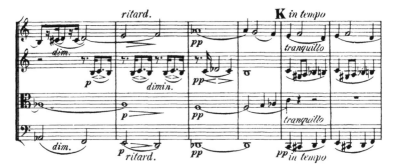

L

II.

Poco Adagio e molto cantabile.

24

D

E

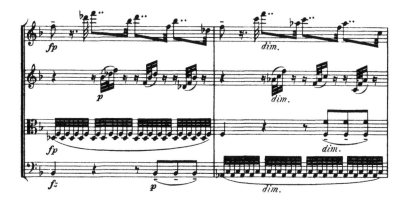

III.
SCHERZO.

Allegro vivo.

Trio.
L'istesso tempo.

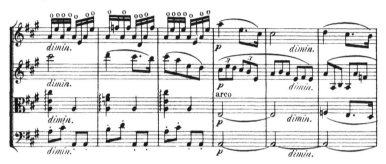

Scherzo D. C. al Fine.

IV.

FINALE.

Vivace.

D

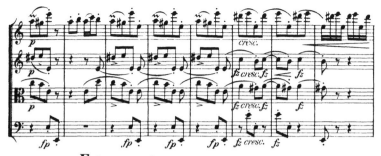

54

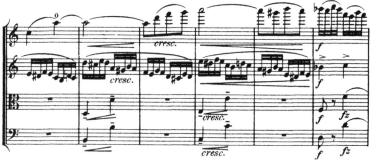

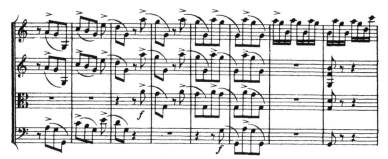